Family Walks around Ski[illegible]

by
Howard M. Beck

Dalesman Books
1990

THE DALESMAN PUBLISHING COMPANY LTD.,
CLAPHAM, via Lancaster, LA2 8EB

First published 1990

ISBN: 0 85206 999 5

Printed by Peter Fretwell & Sons Ltd., Keighley, West Yorkshire BD21 1PZ

CONTENTS

Introduction

MOST travellers to Skipton tend to pass through on route for somewhere else, perhaps heading for the Yorkshire Dales, or even further afield to the Lake District or Scotland. However, as a country market town Skipton has a great deal to delight those prepared to dally, being set amid some fine countryside and nurturing its proud historical heritage.

When I first came to live in Skipton it became apparent that suitable guidebooks on the immediate vicinity were sadly quite lacking. To familiarize myself with the local rural scene I began researching the routes for this book. I soon discovered, to my delight, that I had not been beguiled in my belief that excellent rambling was to be had on the very doorstep as it were.

The result is a collection of walks designed not just for the family group seeking a pleasant afternoon amble, but also for the more seasoned walker wishing to place a respectable number of miles behind him within a single day. The routes described have been graded from two to eleven miles in length, starting with a town trail.

Using Skipton as the focal point most of the walks either start and finish within the town centre or from locations easily reached on foot. Additional walks describe routes a little further afield necessitating the use of public transport or private cars. When required, information regarding bus route numbers is provided; however, since timetables have a habit of changing, the reader is recommended to consult the list of useful addresses and phone numbers contained at the back of this book.

Though it may be somewhat trite to attempt a grading system for walks, I have nevertheless offered some guidance concerning expected duration and difficulties likely to be encountered, particularly with route finding. The most useful map for each walk has been suggested and the scenic value highlighted, and attention has been drawn to historical features encountered along each route. As always, the walker in the countryside should travel prepared for all eventualities, and since some of the routes described cross exposed moorland, the reader is referred to the notes below.

The area covered by this series of walks just touches upon the southernmost fringes of the Yorkshire Dales National Park, and some walks, in particular No.9, may be subject to access limitations at specific times of the year for grouse breeding/

shooting. Other routes described include short sections along 'permissive' pathways where, although not a public right-of-way, walkers are nevertheless tolerated provided they act sensibly. The reader wishing to know more about the area covered in this guide, or to learn about the history of Skipton in more depth, is referred to the bibliography at the end of the book.

FURTHER READING

Biddle, G.	*Pennine Waterway,* Dalesman, 1979.
Bramwell, T.	*About Gargrave,* c.1980.
Brigg, J.J.	*The King's Highway in Craven,* Dixon & Stell, 1927.
Clifford, H.	*The House of Clifford,* Phillimore, 1987.
Dawson, W.H.	*History of Skipton,* 1882.
Ellwood, J.K.	*Life In Old Skipton,* Dalesman, 1982.
Gill, H.	*Ecclesiastical Parish of Gargrave: Vol.1. Flasby,* 1987.
Gray, J.	*Through Airedale from Goole to Malham,* 1891.
Holmes, M.	*Proud Northern Lady.* Phillimore, 1973, reprinted 1984.
Mason, R.	*The Great Skipton Show,* Peter Davies, 1979.
Naylor, R.	*Carleton with an 'E'.* c.1985.
Ordnance Survey	*Map of Roman Britain* (4th Edition), 1978.
Raistrick, A.	*The Pennine Dales,* Eyre & Spottiswoode, 1968.
Raistrick, A.	*Romans in Yorkshire,* Dalesman, 1972.
Rowley, R.G.	*Old Skipton,* Dalesman, 1969.
Rowley, R.G.	*The Book of Skipton,* Barracuda Books, 1983.
Speakman, C.	*Portrait of North Yorkshire,* Hale, 1986.
Whitaker, T.D.	*The History and Antiquities of the Deanery of Craven,* 1805. Reprinted 1973.
Williams, D.	*Medieval Skipton,* Craven District Council, 1981.
Williams, D.	*Excavations at Gargrave (1977-81),* 1983.
Williams, K.	*The History of Lothersdale.* Parish Council of Lothersdale, 1972.
Wright, G.N.	*The Yorkshire Dales,* David & Charles, 1986.

SKIPTON MARKET TOWN

SKIPTON stands at an important geographical junction where roads, canal and railway have all contrived to provide the town with its popular appellation of the 'Gateway to the Dales'. This fact is not attributed to mere accident, for the town owes its strategic importance to its fortuitous location on an east-west break in the Pennine hills known as the Aire Gap, named after the river flowing slightly west of Skipton.

Travellers from the very earliest times to the present have taken full advantage of this natural corridor through the 'Backbone of Britain'. The Romans for instance were very much aware of the Aire Gap, for their surveyors brought a military road this way during the 1st century A.D. Linking Eboracum (York) with Coccium (Ribchester), this came across the shoulder of Skipton Moor, dropping to the site of the town by way of Short Bank Road and passing along an alignment close to that of Newmarket Street. Leaving the town possibly along the line of the now disused railway line to Colne, the Romans took their road through the Aire Gap by way of Broughton. To safeguard the route they built a fort at Burwens near Elslack.

At the time of the Norman Conquest, there was already an Anglian farmstead established where Skipton stands today. This we know from the -ton component of the name, which in the Domesday Book is little different to the current spelling. These settlers probably built their community in the angle of Eller Beck where the latter sweeps around the base of Skipton Rock. With a simple stockade, defence of the site would then have been improved.

Following the Conquest a feudal system was introduced by the overlords which dictated the need for regular markets, and the earliest of these was almost always established beneath the protective cover of the Norman strongholds. At Skipton the first stone edifice was probably erected in 1080 by Robert de Romille following the accession of William I, but there would almost certainly have been an earlier motte and bailey castle on the same site. This would have taken the form of a central mound, the motte, upon which would have been erected a wooden keep. Surrounding this was an earthen ditch and banking surmounted by a timber palisade called a bailey. The remains of the Castle Ditch can in fact be still seen across the A59 from the bailey wall (see the Town Trail). The castle itself is today one of the best preserved examples dating from the Norman period, still fully covered over and now owned by the Fattorini family. The present structure is principally the result of extensive rebuilding at the discretion of Lady Anne Clifford following the siege of the Civil War which ended on 21st December, 1645.

During the 11th and 12th centuries, the Normans to a degree redressed the 'scorched earth' policy they imposed upon the North by founding many abbeys and bestowing upon these religious houses vast tracts of land throughout the Dales. In 1120 Cicely de Romille founded an Augustinian priory at nearby Embsay, and after this was translated to Bolton 35 years afterwards, the Canons were granted the liberty of being exempt from all dues and levies within the town of Skipton.

Trade flourished and the town was given its first market charter in 1203, when regular marts were then a feature of the broad High Street presided over by the castle. One religious order, the Cistercians, were skilled in sheep farming and metal smelting. It was their ability to tame the wild fell country given them by the feudal lords that became a major factor which, combined with the happy circumstances of geography, was responsible for the growth of Skipton into the bustling modern market town. Continuing its tradition as the oldest chartered market town in Airedale, regular markets are still held and remain one of the major attractions for visitors and local communities alike.

From the close of the 18th century, Skipton began to feel the effects of the Industrial Revolution. The harnessing of steam power and improved water-wheel designs resulted in a growth in textiles, and a number of cotton spinning mills sprang up in the town. Increasing demands within the industry brought the Leeds and Liverpool Canal and the Keighley to Kendal Turnpike. The railways soon followed and by the late 19th century, Skipton had a population in the order of 12,000. The largest mill in town at that time was run by John Dewhurst and Sons in Broughton Road employing around 1,000 workers.

With roads continually improving, the significance of the railways has much diminished and the canal, long since forsaken as an industrial artery, now merely forms another tourist backwater, plied seasonally by a miscellany of pleasure craft. The town centre is itself pleasantly compact with no steep hills, forming an ideal centre for the visitor seeking little more strenuous than a shopping outing. In this respect Skipton offers an exciting venue, steeped in historical associations and presenting many interesting examples of vernacular architecture reflecting several periods.

Tasteful redevelopment of the town's centre areas has resulted in a relaxed shopping atmosphere that is never very far from the serene reaches of the Leeds to Liverpool Canal or the sylvan depths of Castle Woods. The opening of a much needed by-pass means visitors can now browse at leisure relatively free of the traffic congestion that was once a feature of the town. Once away from the usual market day clamour of the broad High Street, the visitor will by contrast discover a hotch-potch of yards and narrow ginnels that in the past once echoed to the staccato sound of countless clogged feet. He or she may saunter at will through Victoria Square or Craven Court, a recently opened shopping mall focussing upon a surviving medieval street reminiscent of York's famous Shambles.

As a centre for outdoor activities, Skipton is a paragon without equal, its reputation for salubrity vested in its proximity to the southern fringe of the Yorkshire Dales National Park. Although ideally positioned as a 'springboard' from which to launch expeditions to this fine region, or nearby Brontë Country or Pendle, the reader should not allow this fact to overshadow the attributes of the surrounding countryside. Rock climbing is to be had at Crookrise Crag two miles north of town, whilst the highest points of the adjacent fells provide some dramatic panoramas. As a final task it now remains only for me to wish the reader enjoyable walking, hope that the use of this book increases the pleasure, and trust in his or her safe return.

Opening Times

Skipton Castle is open daily (except Christmas Day) from 10 a.m. (2 p.m. Sunday) until 6 p.m., or sunset if this is earlier.

Craven Museum opens Monday to Friday (except Tuesday) from 1st April to 30th September from 11 a.m. to 5 p.m. (Sunday 2 p.m. to 5 p.m.; Saturday 10 a.m. to 12 noon and 1 p.m. to 5 p.m.). Admission free.

WALK 1

TOWN TRAIL

Distance: 2 miles. Expected duration 1 hour. Add more if time is to be spent in the museum and castle.

STARTING from the central car park, walk back toward the High Street where a right turn here passes the entrance to the Craven Museum and Town Hall. In the days when the High Street was still used as a stock market the thoroughfare got into such a state that a raised pavement was provided from the church gate to the vicarage, the latter originally existing where the Town Hall now stands. Remains of the pavement can be seen in the setts outside the Town Hall building.

A short distance further up the High Street is a fine building called The Bailey. This was once the fashionable residence of Henry Alcock but is now the premises of a firm of solicitors. Just beyond this house and across the road is the gateway to the castle, above which may be seen the Clifford family motto Desormais (Hereafter). Skipton Castle is without doubt one of the best preserved Norman strongholds in the country. The present structure was a result of rebuilding and extension by the Cliffords between 1311 and 1676 which included the Tudor Wing and Octagonal Tower.

The first stone-built structure was erected by 1080 at the command of Robert de Romille, although it is fairly certain that this was predated by a timber and earth Motte and Bailey. During the Civil War the castle remained under siege of Parliamentary troops for three years and was extensively damaged by cannon fire from what is now Castle Street. Cromwell also had a battery of cannon set up on Park Hill a quarter mile to the north-west.

From the castle gate take the path east up the road known as The Bailey, following the high perimeter wall of the castle bailey itself. As one ascends gently, note the section of ditch in the field across the road. Known as castle ditch, this is possibly a surviving part of earthworks associated with the first motte and bailey defensive structure. At the second set of stone steps descend to and cross the road to enter Rectory Lane, walking down this for some 400 yards.

At the cross-roads with Otley Street turn to the right and proceed as far as the Albion public house, where a left turn

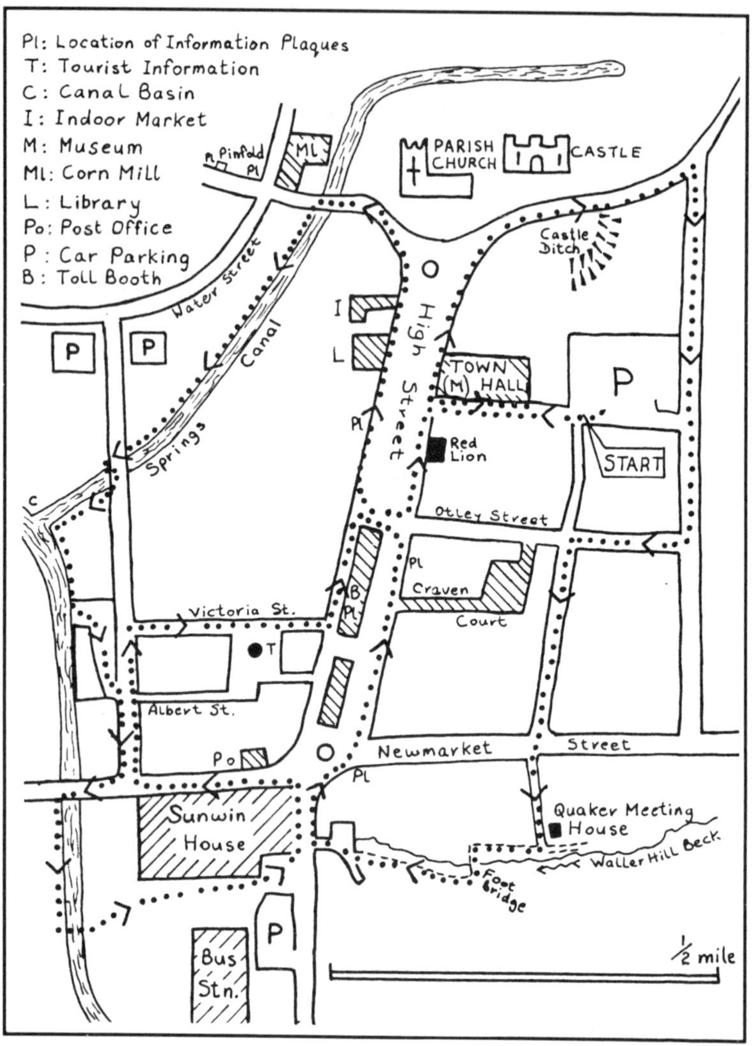

outside the entrance to the Craven Court shopping centre takes one along Court Lane to Newmarket Street. The latter follows the approximate line of the old York to Lancaster coach road which came down into town via the steep hill of Shode Bank (Short Bank) Road, itself a route adopting the course of the Roman military highway from Eboracum (York) to Coccium (Ribchester). A number of Roman coins were in fact unearthed along the south side of Newmarket Street.

From Court lane cross Newmarket Street into The Ginnel and walk along this past the 17th century Quaker Meeting House on the left. Turn right at the end, along a pathway soon crossing Waller Hill Beck by a footbridge to trace the far bank. It is commonly thought that the town ducking stool was once sited close to this bridge. Still tracing the beck until eventually it enters culvert, walk past Skipton Car Radio premises and the Unicorn Hotel building to the junction with Keighley Road.

Turn right here to the old Ship Corner at the junction with Swadford Street, bearing around to the right into what was formerly known as Caroline Square situated at the foot of the High Street and the parallel Sheep Street. Affixed to the wall between Woolworths and Superdrug Store can be seen a round stone tablet. This commemorates that in 1851 Thomas Spencer, co-founder of the Marks and Spencer Group, was born in a house once standing on this site, an ironic twist for a town which does not benefit from one of their stores!

Proceeding now up the right-hand side of the High Street, pass a second entrance to the Craven Court, a recent development centred upon a medieval street. When Barclays Bank is reached, note that in front of this building once stood the town pillory (removed in 1770) as well as the market cross and stocks (removed in 1840). At the intersection with Otley Street, cross the high Street by Manby's Corner, until recently the family ironmongery business established here in 1817 and now a shop retailing woolies. At the Yorkshire Bank once stood the Bay Horse Inn, and a plaque on the bank wall states that in front was the bull baiting stone. A further 50 yards up the street is the library and Craven College buildings, in front of which stands the statue of Sir Mathew Wilson, MP for the West Riding Northern Division (1874-1885) and who later became the first MP for the Skipton district.

Continuing up the High Street toward the Parish Church, pass the Black Horse, an ancient hostelry said by local tradition to have been a Royal Mews of Richard III from 1583 to 1585, when he was Lord of the castle and Honour of Skipton. To the left of the main entrance is a fine example of mounting steps, whilst set in the wall above these can be seen a strange carved stone bearing what appear like boars' heads. The latter were featured on the Royal Standard of King Richard but the stone is dated 1676.

After contemplating the pedigree and charm of the Black Horse, proceed past the entrance to Mount Pleasant to the retail premises of David Goldie. This double-fronted former Georgian residence was the birthplace of John McMoran, later Lord Moran, who distinguished himself by becoming the personal physician to Sir Winston Churchill. The Parish Church is now just the opposite side of the road. The earliest mention of a religious house on this spot is for the year 1120, though it is widely thought that the Angles who founded the town must also have built a church. The structure was rebuilt in the 14th century and enlarged in the 15th, but during the height of Civil War had its tower severely damaged by a stray cannon ball meant for the castle. The foundation stone for the present building was laid in 1837, and despite the ravages of time the Clifford family vault still survives beneath the altar.

Strolling round the bend to Mill Bridge, walk to where the road spans Springs Canal and Eller Beck, noting the latter running from beneath the High Corn Mill. A mill is known to have co-existed with the castle at this spot since quite early times and mention of it was made in a valuation document dated 1310. It was until very recently a working mill and folk museum run by George Leatt. The York to Lancaster highway once forded Eller Beck at this point, which together with the church and castle was in about 1300 the centre of town.

From the bridge descend the stone steps on its south side and walk for 300 yards along the canal towpath as far as Coach Street bridge. Walk beneath this and climb the narrow flight of steps on the right back to the road, turning immediately right. Cross the bridge and take the first right, walking down to the canal basin, a hive of narrow boat activity in the high season. Follow the Leeds to Liverpool Canal around to the left and from here enter the cobbled yard fronting the Dales Outdoor Centre, housed in a former waterside warehouse complete with the derricks once used to load the barges.

From the yard enter and turn right along Coach Street, turning right at the end to Belmont Bridge. Cross the road at this point to find some steps leading once more down to the towpath. Walk along to the footbridge seen in front and cross this to enter a car park area adjacent to Sunwin House. Walking past the latter reach Keighley Road and, turning left here, reach the corner with Swadford Street. This is one of the oldest thoroughfares in Skipton and takes its name from an ancient ford which once existed nearby.

Walk left along Swadford Street passing the ancient public house of the Cock and Bottle, probably the only building along this street still retaining something of its character, then turn into Coach Street again. A short distance past the Rose and Crown turn right up Victoria Street, passing the new Tourist Information building and soon afterwards entering Sheep Street. Turning left here note the Gift Emporium up the steps on the right. This was formerly the town hall and toll booth, beneath which were the cells where felons were imprisoned and branded. At the base of the steps leading up into the building are remains of the stocks at either side. It was on these very steps on 16th August 1842, that Mathew Wilson read out the Riot Act to a gathering mob of predominantly Lancastrian 'wreckers' who had marched upon Skipton seeking support in their opposition to the introduction of power in the mills.

Continue up Sheep Street to Manby's Corner and from here cross the high Street and proceed up the opposite side. Note the Red Lion public house. This building is said to stand where from 1310 to 1350 existed a leper hospital of St. Mary Magdalene. An inn has been here since then, making the Red Lion one of the oldest buildings in town. A few yards up the High Street is the right turn by Whitakers confectioners leading back to the central car park.

WALK 2

SKIPTON WOOD - PARK HILL - CHAPEL HILL

Distance 2.25 miles with an anticipated duration of one-and-a-half hours. Easy walking on good paths with very little uphill work. Landranger Map No. 103 (Blackburn and Burnley) is required.

This walk starts at Mill Bridge close to the Parish Church; however, visitors to Skipton may leave their car at the car park adjacent to the old fire station building at the north end of Coach Street. This building housed the Skipton Fire Brigade until 1974; prior to this it was a cycle shop and even earlier it was the first Primitive Methodist Chapel from 1835 to 1880.

FROM the car park turn right along Coach Street as far as the hump back bridge over Springs Canal, but just before this on the left take a right-of-way which leads immediately on to the towpath. Walk along this for about 200 yards with the church clock tower visible ahead. Passing beneath Mill bridge enter a lawned area between the canal and Eller Beck, where the latter is seen flowing from beneath the old mill building. The latter is now the new home of quality household furnishers Ledgard and Wynn.

The way forward continues as a raised footway sandwiched between the cut and the beck, where at a number of places water is seen cascading down the high banking to the left. These are spill channels from the Long Dam, constructed above and parallel to Eller Beck, which once formed part of the water supply for both the High Corn Mill and Dewhursts Mill in Broughton Road. As the pathway wends its way around the back of Skipton Castle the viewpoint presents a less common but nonetheless impressive aspect of the stronghold. Perched in a seemingly precarious fashion high upon Skipton Rock it is easy to see why the Normans chose this site for a defensive placement. From the battlements it is a sheer 200 ft drop down to the beck. Look closely too at the rock beneath the castle and see the strata of the limestone twisted and folded by immense geological forces.

Just past the castle the end of Springs Canal is reached, and here we can see the surviving chutes at the foot of what once was an inclined tramway. Limestone quarried at nearby Haw Bank was transported to this point for loading into barges for shipping to various parts of the country. Eller Beck is here spanned by a footbridge, and crossing this a right turn leads on to a driveway into a private garden. This is now a concession access through to Skipton Woods (open daily 2-7 pm between May 1st and September 30th and until 6 pm or sunset at other dates) so please observe the signs and keep to the paths provided.

At the end of the garden pass through a gate and cross a small wooden bridge, a few yards beyond which the route meets Sandy Goit. A left turn at this point follows the water channel to where it has been diverted down under the bridge just crossed; however, the former course of the goit can still be seen where this continued to the waterwheels of the mills.

Returning to the main path, follow this now for half-a-mile through delightful broadleaf woodlands with the beck flowing noisily in a ravine down to the right. These pathways through

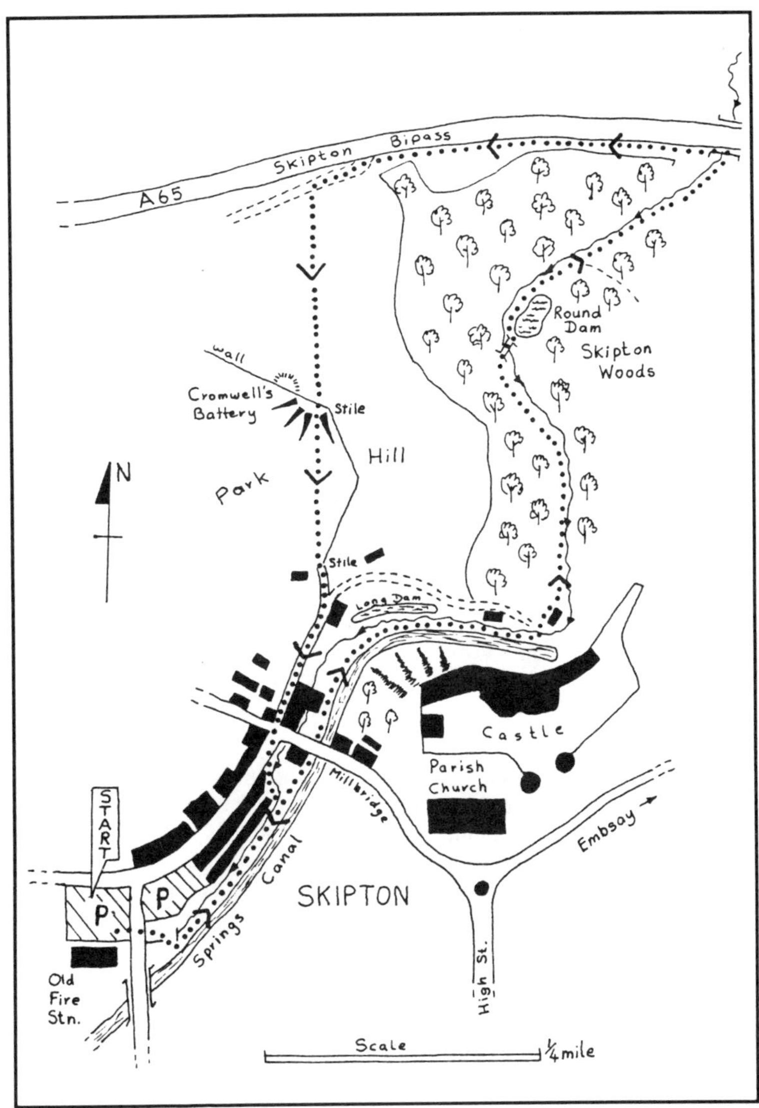

the woods originally formed an ornamental pleasure garden enjoyed by the Cliffords. Sandy Goit soon ends where a metal bridge spans Eller Beck and immediately beyond is the so-called Round Dam. A close inspection of the bridge structure quickly reveals that this is supported by the aqueduct which conveys water from the dam into Sandy Goit.

Although obviously artificial the dam is now given over completely to nature and its immediate environs are an absolute haven for birdlife and wild flowers. It is difficult to imagine the scene as anything other than the picture of tranquillity; however, in 1908 it was quickly transformed to a scene of utter devastation when torrential rain caused the dam to burst its banks. The floodwaters wreaked havoc downstream and the towpath along Springs Canal was some four feet underwater. Time heals all wounds however and the shoreline of this serene pool is in springtime ablaze with marsh marigolds and other blooms, whilst the first visitors of the day may — if they are quiet — be treated to chance encounters with the shy heron, or catch sight of woodpeckers and nuthatches.

Just to the left of the Round Dam are the surviving sluice gates and a weir where the water supply to the dam could be varied according to need. Level walking now leaves the noise of the weir behind as the beck traces a more sedate course. Very soon, though, the watercourse is squeezed through a narrowing of the banks where the stream has carved a way through the upturned beds of locally outcropping limestone. Not many yards beyond here the beck has been culverted beneath the A59 Skipton by-pass. The path continues though, and passing behind the twin culverts it can be traced as it angles left up the slope of the banking to follow a course parallel but safely to one side of this busy road.

Level walking once again prevails, at first alongside a dry-stone wall, but where this gives way to a fence after half-a-mile, the path then gradually descends to a farm access lane at a stile (note fingerpost). From this stile cross the lane and by a step stile enter the field opposite and follow the path uphill. When the wall is reached at the top of Park Hill a step stile is found; however, before crossing this walk up the wall side for some 40 yards to the right and here find the vaguely square outline of an earthwork bisected by the wall. This dates from the time of the Civil War and by tradition is said to be one of the sites where Cromwell set up his cannon during the siege of Skipton Castle.

Returning now to the stile, dwell awhile upon the superb view across the town with Skipton Moor as a backcloth and the Aire Valley receding into the distance. From the stile walk down the hill heading for the bottom left corner where a further stile leads into a descending lane. Follow this to the junction with Chapel Hill by the former Wesleyan Chapel building, and by turning left here and walking on for a few yards a glimpse over the wall on the right offers a view of the Long Dam.

Back at the junction proceed down the hill to Raikes Road at the bottom. At one side are the High Corn Mill buildings, outside which is a fine example of a horse-in-stone once used to mount horses before the advent of the motor car. At the far side of the street a small cottage facing into Chapel Hill bears a plaque on the wall which announces that on the 26th June 1764 John Wesley preached to the townsfolk close to this point.

The road junction stands roughly on the site of the town pinfold. This was an enclosure where a specially appointed person, known as a pinder, would impound animals found straying. The owners of the offending beasts could reclaim them only upon payment of the appropriate fine. From this junction, cross now into Water Street and walk along this for 80 yards to the cycle shop. Just before this follow a right-of-way down to the left called Back O'the Beck to reach a footbridge over Eller Beck. Cross this and turn right once more following the canal towpath. At Coach Street a right turn returns the walker back to the car park by the old fire station.

WALK 3

KILDWICK AND FARNHILL MOOR

Distance 3.5 miles. Allow one-and-a-half hours for this walk.

This easy stroll, ideal for the odd half day, starts and ends along a two-mile stretch of the Leeds to Liverpool canal, where the latter passes through the twin Domesday villages of Fernehil (Farnhill) and Childeuuic (Kildwick). Climbing northwards out of Kildwick, the route then crosses parts of Farnhill Moor where ancient earthworks are to be found.

You will require Landranger Map Sheet 104 (Leeds and Bradford).

THIS walk commences at a pulling-off space located (SE 003470) beside the A629 at Cononley Lane end, passed also by West Yorkshire bus service No. 666.

From the lay-by and bus stop, walk up the overgrown banking on to the canal towpath and follow this south in the direction of Kildwick, very soon passing under the road bridge, often referred to as Vietnam Bridge owing to graffiti once decorating the spandrel walls. Walking along a rather pleasant section of this busy inland waterway, where tree cover descends from the slopes of Farnhill Moor, very soon Farnhill Hall can be seen up to the left. This imposing residence with its castellated turrets is said to date from the time of the Norman Conquest when it was a manor in the parish of Kildwick, though doubtless the present structure stands where an earlier building once stood. According to another local tradition a passage once passed from the cellars of Farnhill Hall to Royd House on the other side of the valley, even though his would have had to pass beneath the river!

Having emerged from the tree cover and passing the first swing bridge, the canal then bends around to the right and the residences of Farnhill come into view, clinging fortress-like to the hillside overlooking the valley. Looking southwards from here Sutton and nearby Glusburn can be seen presided over by Earl Crag and the tower of Wainman Pinnacle. After passing a canalside warehouse building that has been converted to residential uses, a second bridge is met beyond which the clock tower of Kildwick church can be seen. Do not cross the canal at this point, but continue where the canal is carried on an aqueduct over Kirkgate, part of the old pre-turnpike route between Keighley and Kendal.

When the stone bridge is reached spanning the canal, pass through the iron gate here, turn left up the steps and then turning down to the right follow a path to the church. The village of Kildwick is extremely ancient for we know from the Domesday records that land here was held by the Anglo-Saxon Arnketill. The church too, popularly known as the Lang Kirk o'Craven, is one of only two to be given a mention in the Domesday Survey for this area. The church is a workwhile diversion from our little sojourn and around it are contained many interesting and curious tombstones. At the Priestbank Road entrance to the churchyard, opposite the White Lion public house, is a memorial to the menfolk who fell in the Second World War. Immediately behind this, within shrubbery covering the banking, is the village stocks. Inside too are many notable features, not least of them being the Norman font.

Returning to the stone bridge, cross this to the lich gate leading

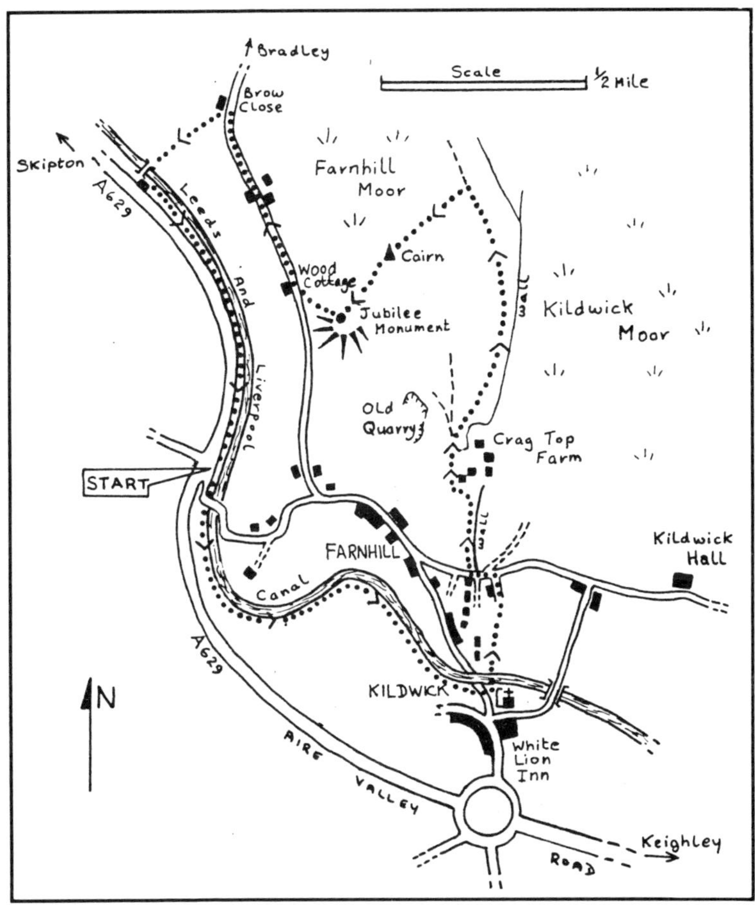

to an additional graveyard but take the flagged pathway on the left and trace this for almost quarter of a mile uphill to a gate. From here a field path continues, still paved, and after about 60 yards reaches a second gate where the path merges with a lane by the vicarage. The lane through High Farnhill is soon met at the top, where to the right within 300 yards is the entrance to the Jacobean mansion of Kildwick Hall, now functioning as a restaurant of some repute. There is an endearing local tale regarding the stone lions guarding the main entrance, which according to legend descend to the river Aire at midnight to slake their thirst.

To continue now for Farnhill Moor, turn left along the lane

where it is first encountered and walk along a short way to a bend where Starkey Lane goes off left. Opposite this pick up a footpath (signposted Farnhill Moor) and trace the wall side for about quarter of a mile to Crag Top Farm. Bear over to the left here, around to the left of the buildings to reach a stile by a gate. A few yards beyond this the path branches three ways. Taking the one trending half right around a wall corner, follow it for quarter of a mile as it steadily climbs on to the open moor. Passing through a scattered growth of immature silver birch, bracken and ling, a large pointed cairn soon becomes visible over to the left.

Continue along the path to the first obvious branch leading left and follow this as the way forward levels out to the cairn. Although of no particular vintage, this impressive structure stands 12 ft tall and is in the region of 8 ft across at its base. Other cairns and earthworks possibly dating from the Bronze Age are to be found about quarter of a mile to the north and north-east of this site.

Continue along the well-defined pathway from the cairn to reach the Jubilee Monument seen ahead, erected in honour of Queen Victoria. It is surmounted by a stone cross dated 1887 and bearing images of a rose, thistle and a shamrock. The location commands a fine prospect of Airedale extending from Rivock Edge by Keighley up dale to Malham Moors and Sharp Haw. Just a few feet on the valley side of the monument is a low boulder with the inscription . . . 'and was restored on the occasion of the silver jubilee of King George V, May 6 1935, God Save the King'.

By the side of this stone a path then descends a rocky course from Farnhill Crag threading its way through heather towards the woods at the foot of the moor. Dropping down through birch woods the old pre-turnpike road is soon joined by Wood Cottage. Turning right here, walk up the lane for a little over quarter of a mile to find a stile on the left a few yards before Brow Close Farm. A public bridleway can now be traced downhill across pastures, passing through a gate at the far side of the first field, and from there heading for the bottom left corner where a second gate leads quickly to the canal and a bridge. Crossing at this point a left turn and three-quarters of a mile of easy walking returns to the starting point near Vietnam Bridge.

WALK 4

EMBSAY RESERVOIR AND CROOKRISE TOP

Distance 4.25 miles.

An ideal venue for a balmy summer evening stroll which can be completed with a couple of hours. The walk starts and returns to the Elm Tree public house in Embsay (5 minutes drive from Skipton, or public transport: West Yorkshire bus No. 276 or Pennine No. 214).

The most useful map coverage is unfortunately taken up by two sheets, being Nos. 103 and 104 in the O.S. Landranger Series or SD 85/95 and SE 05/15 Pathfinder Maps.

FROM the Elm Tree pub, walk along the road east and within 50 yards or so turn into the car park on the left. Here a ladder stile leads directly upon a field path running alongside a wall by a barn. Aim for the gap stile over to the right, and from this point follow the path for 60 yards between a wall and a wire fence.

At the next gap stile the continuing path leads to the far left corner of the following field, where the lane is entered and followed to the left. Shortly after passing the tiny church an acute bend in the road turns east and some 50 yards later reaches the entrance to Hodson Farmhouse (B & B). Just beyond this turn left up a public bridleway (signposted Embsay Crag and Reservoir) and follow this uphill for quarter of a mile to a farm entrance where the pathway continues straight forward over a ladder stile.

A green track is now traced, still ascending with a stream flowing in a ravine down on the left. Almost quarter of a mile later the way becomes a walled lane soon leading to a gate. From here bear left and walk up the wall side with the jutting prow of Embsay Crag visible over to the left. At the top left corner of the pasture pass through a gate and turn left. Following the wall side now and passing a sheep fold, a well-defined track winds its way up through chest-high bracken to the summit of Embsay Crag.

Although of modest elevation this top enjoys an excellent view, not only taking in the nearest settlements but beyond

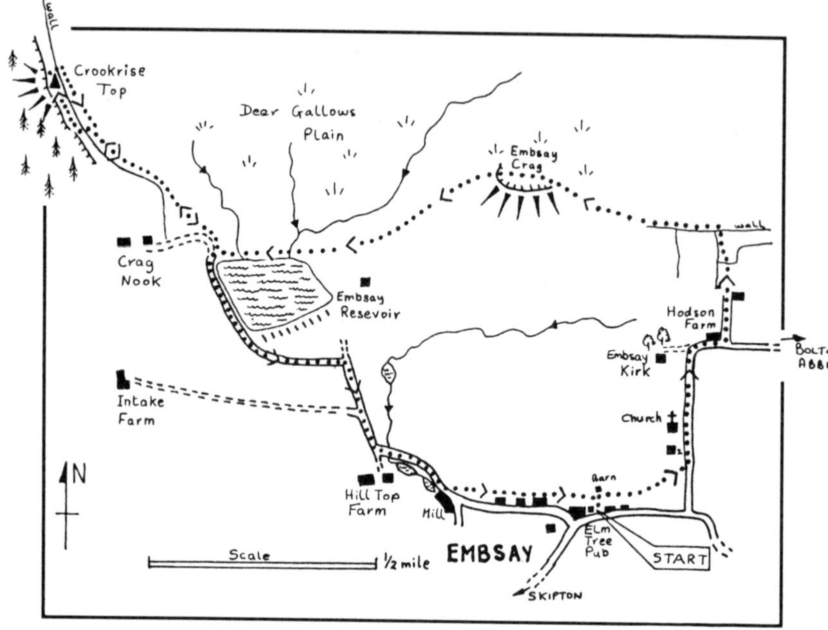

Skipton to the receding Aire Valley and Elslack Moor across the Aire Gap. After savouring the panorama from this gritty height, trace the continuation of the bridleway as it descends steeply, once again through a jungle of bracken, eventually crossing a stream at a footbridge. From here walk along the north side of the reservoir following a track to a stile.

Do not cross here but trace the fence uphill to the right to reach a wall side. Follow this up the hill for quarter of a mile towards Saddle Holes, then with an ever steepening gradient as far as a ladder stile. An easy level pathway continues forward; however, by crossing the wall at the stile a route can be traced as it wanders along the base of Crookrise Crags, before ascending to return to Crag Nook via a second ladder stile near the O.S. trig. point and High Edge.

Crookrise Crag is a very popular gritstone edge visited regularly by climbers on most weekends and evenings in summer. The Yorkshire Ramblers' Club pioneered routes here as early as 1923 and the site is historically regarded as where outcrop climbing in Yorkshire all began.

It is a well weathered escarpment of millstone grit where in the past stone was quarried for local building work and millstones. On almost any visit ramblers may be treated to the sight of rock gymnasts at play on such classic routes as Griffith's Chimney, Flake Wall, Hovis, Sole and many more.

Ascending now through the outcrop and boulders to reach the stile at Crookrise Top, cross the wall and turn right walking back along the wall down to the stile at Crag Nook. From here take the track around the west side of the reservoir and follow this until it becomes the metalled Pasture Road. Soon after the mill dams are reached look for an obscure step stile up to the left. Go through this and walk up the wall on the right for a few yards to another stile.

From here a well-defined field path is followed for somewhat over quarter of a mile, passing on route several enclosure walls by way of stiles. The path soon passes to the rear of the school; beyond here and a fence corner aim for a fingerpost where a stile can be found. A ladder stile at the bottom (right-hand side) of the next field takes the walker back to the car park near to the Elm Tree pub.

WALK 5

STIRTON AND THORLBY VILLAGES

Distance 4.75 miles. Expected duration between 1-2 hours.

This is an easy stroll taking in sections of the Leeds and Liverpool Canal and hamlets dating from the Dark Ages.

Landranger Map No. 103 (Blackburn and Burnley) is required.

Visitors may leave their cars at the railway station car park in Broughton Road. Alternatively start the walk at Belmont Bridge near the town centre.

LEAVING the railway station car park, cross Broughton Road and walk up the lane immediately opposite (signposted Aireville Park and Swimming Pool). Cross the swing bridge over the canal where walkers starting at Belmont Bridge join the route. Turn sharp left by Aireville Nurseries to follow the canalside pathway for half-a-mile bordering woods, eventually reaching a gate where the canal swings southwards.

Once through the gate, pass through the next one immediately

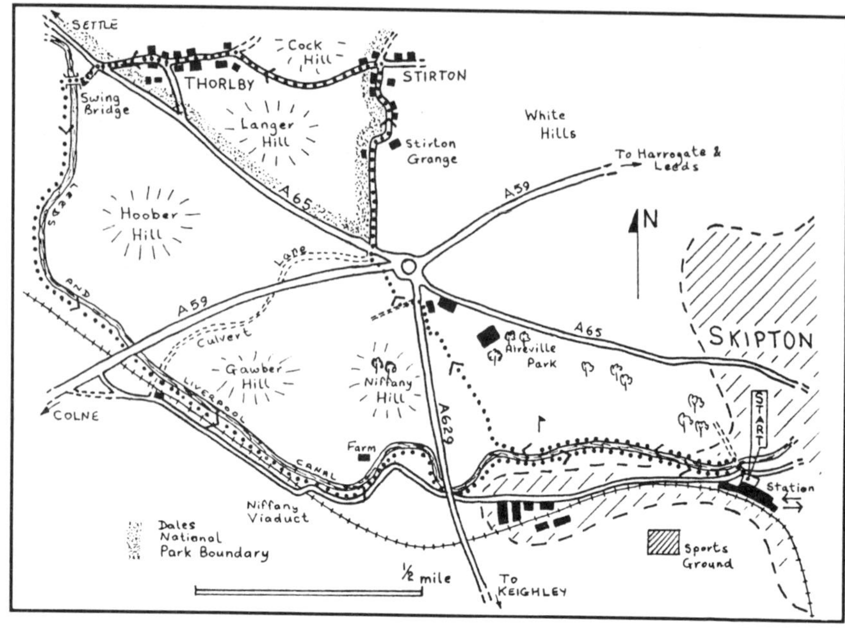

on the right and head for a stile leading into playing fields. Strike across the latter aiming for the far left corner where a stile is crossed to enter a farm track by a gate. Pass through this taking the field path and keeping to the right-hand edge to reach another gate. Here turn sharp left, walking alongside the hedgerow until a fence is met at the by-pass.

Turn right, at this point walking parallel to the road (look for the yellow waymarking arrows) and after 50 yards pass through a line of thorn bushes. Still keeping to the fence, walk along the rear of the warehouse building to reach a stile at a wall corner. Pass through this and with care cross the busy by-pass to another stile at the far side. From here an ascending overgrown track is followed between thorn trees until some 30 yards later a path branches off on the right tracing a shallow dip flanked by tree stumps. Cross a stile within 60 yards and follow the path as it angles down to and crosses the by-pass yet again. From here Sharp Haw can be seen immediately in front with the gritty scarp of Crookrise Crags to the right.

Once safely across this road and over the next stile, walk down the wall side to a gate at the bottom leading into a farm track. Turning to the right here and crossing the A65, follow the narrow lane (signposted to Stirton) for about quarter of a mile, noting the quaint 17th century cottage on the left and soon entering the hamlet. The "-ton" suffix of this place-name is indicative that here was a settlement originally established by the Angles.

At the cross-roads in the centre of the hamlet look out for the remains of the village stocks partially concealed in the grass verge. After contemplating the punishments that were undoubtedly meted out on this spot in the past, turn left towards the hamlet of Thorlby. Once again we have here an example of the way in which place-names can be diagnostic of early settlement. In this instance the component offering the clue is "-by", evidence that this hamlet grew from a group of settling Danes probably during the 9th century.

From the cross-roads at Stirton it is a pleasant half-a-mile amble into Thorlby where the narrow lane is found to divide. Bearing right here takes the walker back once more to the A65, but crossing this a short track soon meets the Leeds and Liverpool Canal. Cross the bridge and turn left, now following the original towpath used by ponies to pull laden barges to the ports of Merseyside. After a little over a mile reach Broughton Road, where the walker must leave the canal side momentarily, turning left along the road, but reaching the towpath again after 200 yards. After passing beneath the flyover a further three-quarters of a mile of walking leads back to the lane where turning to the right quickly reaches the starting point by the railway station.

WALK 6

SKIPTON MOOR AND CAWDER GILL

Distance 6 miles. Expected duration for average walkers about two-and-a-half hours.

This route presents no great difficulties but as it crosses open fell, suitable foul weather precautions should be taken. The walk offers some excellent views out over the town, and the starting and finishing point is the central bus station.

You will need Landranger Series Map Nos. 103 and 104.

LEAVING the bus station by way of the Keighley Road exit, adjacent to the public convenience block, cross the road and walk up Sackville Street to where this sweeps around to the right at the end. At this point carry straight on up the hill of upper Sackville Street crossing the railway line. A pathway from here cuts alongside playing fields before descending to a gate at a housing estate. Turn left here along Pinhaw Road to its junction with North Parade by the school.

Cross the road and carry on straight forward over a stile and ascend a footpath heading for the open moors. With a dry-stone wall on the right and a stream gulley on the left, trace the path uphill for 130 yards to a step stile in a wall corner. About 20 yards beyond this, turn left along a farm track to pass another stile by a gate after a further 50 yards. Continuing along the wall side with a radio repeater mast over on the right, descend quickly to another stile and gate to join a stony track at a sweeping bend. Ignore this to carry straight forward into a housing estate.

Walk along Whinney Gill Road for 80 yards downhill to a 'T' junction. Turn to the right here, soon followed by a right turn up Short Bank Road now following the course of the former York to Lancaster coaching road. When the metalling peters out continue steeply up through the trees with a wall to the right. After a while the route ahead takes on a braided form, ascending with a greater gradient, but by following a path around to the right, still tracing the wallside, continue uphill around by the old quarry enjoying expansive views over the town. The route levels out around the top end of the wood soon reaching a walled lane, part of the course of the Roman military highway from York to Ribchester.

Ignore the continuing lane and take a gate immediately on the right, and from here ascend the track as it winds up to a stile and gate in a wall corner at the top of the pasture. From this point a pathway cuts across open moorland for about half-a-mile to reach the summit of Skipton Moor. A magnificent panorama unfolds on all sides from the O.S. trig. point and includes Simon's Seat, Crookrise, Sharp Haw and the fells of Bowland.

To continue on our way follow the path along the summit ridge to a cairn 50 yards away, and from here take the clear path that strikes across in a southerly direction over Vicar's Allotment towards a gritstone scarp a short distance away. When this is reached turn right following a path with a wall on the

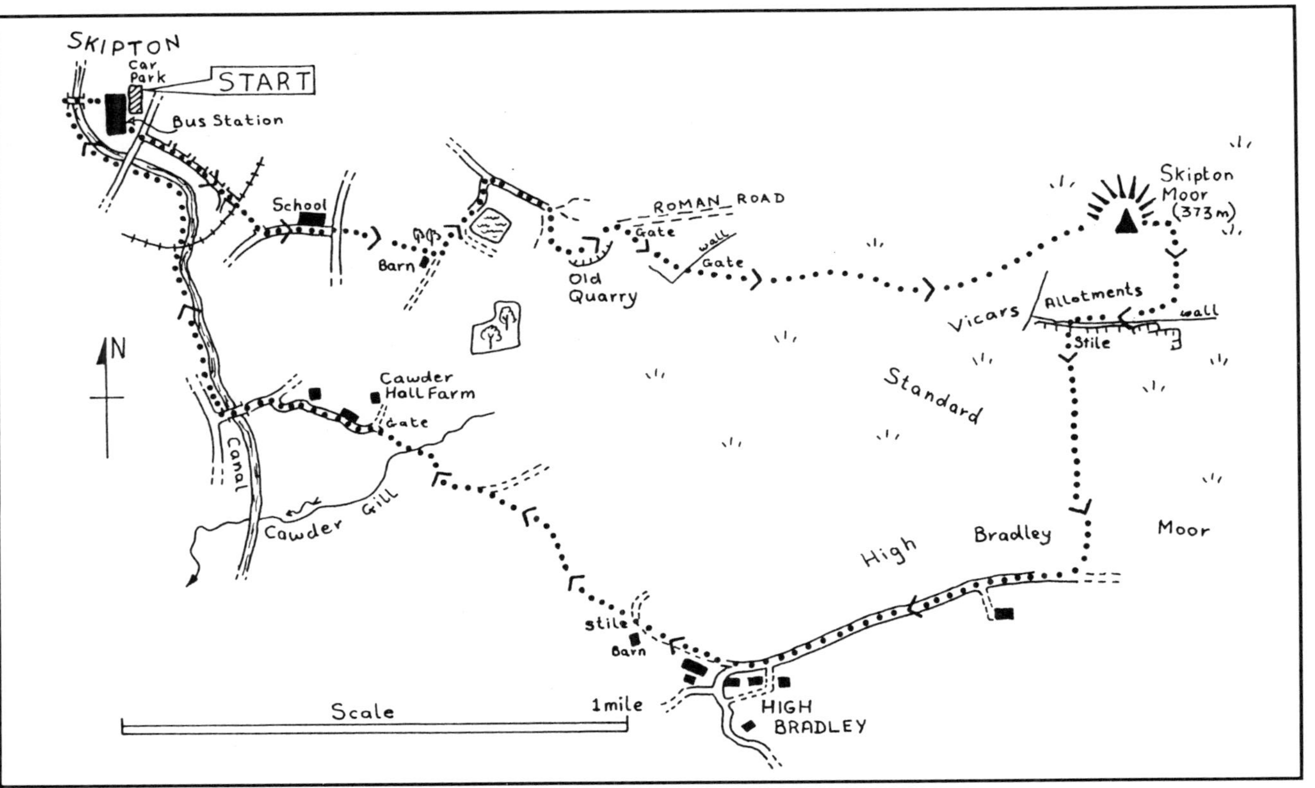
SKIPTON
Car Park
START
Bus Station
School
Barn
ROMAN ROAD
Gate
wall
Gate
Old Quarry
Skipton Moor (373m)
Vicars
Allotments
wall
Stile
N
Cawder Hall Farm
Gate
Standard
Canal
Cawder Gill
High
Bradley
Moor
stile
Barn
Scale
1 mile
HIGH BRADLEY

left as far as a stile after quarter of a mile then turn left. With a wall now to the right, trace a field path across High Bradley Moor eventually descending ever steeper to converge upon a farm track where the latter meets a line of overhead power lines.

Turning to the right (west) along this track High Bradley is reached after three-quarters of a mile of level walking. Soon afterwards the track becomes a tarmac lane and a few yards later another track leaves at a slight tangent and a little higher than the now descending lane. Taking this route go through a gate and walk around the right side of a farmhouse to reach another gate at a wall corner. There is a stile slightly to the right.

From here follow the farm track as it winds around to the right with a barn on the left and follow it for quarter of a mile, to where it swings right uphill. There is a gate immediately ahead but cross the gap stile to the left of this and strike across to the right-hand of two gates seen ahead. Pick up another gap stile at this point and then descend slightly, at first with a wall on the left, but when this turns sharp left cut across the field to a stile in the corner.

By turning half left from here make for the top of a line of thorn trees to find another gate, and stile to the right of it, after which follow a descending farm track to reach yet another gate at Cawder Gill. Through this the track is followed to meet a concrete lane leading uphill to Cawder Hall Farm. From here carry straight on by farm buildings passing Cawder Gill nursing home and after quarter of a mile meeting an intersection with a housing estate road. A left turn here quickly reaches Keighley Road after crossing the canal bridge. Turn right to reach the towpath and walk for a little over three-quarters of a mile back into the town centre. Cross the canal at the footbridge here to return to the bus station and car parking areas at the start of the walk.

WALK 7

RIVER AIRE
AND A DOMESDAY HAMLET

Distance 6.5 miles. Expected duration 3 hours.

This fine route takes in the riverbank scenery of Airedale, the fine vernacular architecture of Cononley village and returns to Skipton along the towpath of the Leeds and Liverpool Canal.

The recommended O.S. map is the Landranger Series sheet 103.

THIS walk commences at Carleton Bridge twenty minutes out of town and a pulling-over spot can be found (SD 983505) a few yards on the Carleton side of the town crematorium. The Pennine Bus company run a service to Carleton (service number 211/212).

Leaving the car at the lay-by, walk along the road in the direction of Carleton, and where the road divides just after the Aire bridge take the left-hand fork (signposted Cononley and Lothersdale) to find a gate and stile leading into the rough pasture on the left. From here the path cuts straight across the field to follow a riverbank route for about one and three-quarter miles. After only half-a-mile the pathway passes beneath the railway to a step stile almost immediately. Beyond this the riverside route continues to wend its way along the alluvial flats of the valley floor. An early morning sojourn along this section of the walk offers hope of chance sightings of heron, kingfishers or sandmartins, the high earthen banks providing an ideal habitat.

Before long a wooden stile is met where the route crosses a fence and, still keeping to the riverbank with the fence now to the right, the path winds around in phase with the river meanders. Some quarter of a mile after the railway bridge a newly built dry-stone wall is reached at a gate close to a culvert leading into the river. Still with the river the path crosses Bradley Ings as far as a point almost due west of Bradley Lane Ends. Look for and follow a farm track that runs off at a slight tangent to the course of the Aire and is flanked with hawthorne trees.

The track merely cuts across a loop in the river and quickly meets the latter once again where a track comes in from the right. Ignore this and follow the riverbank for a further quarter of a mile along the track until more field drainage works are seen. The farm track now takes a sharp turn toward the south-west and for around 400 yards is flanked by hedgerows of blackthorn and haw. The Aire Valley railway line is crossed (care!) and the continuing track, now called Shady Lane, enters Cononley quarter of a mile later. Turn left along Skipton Road to reach the village centre within 250 yards.

Cononley has an interesting pedigree being mentioned in

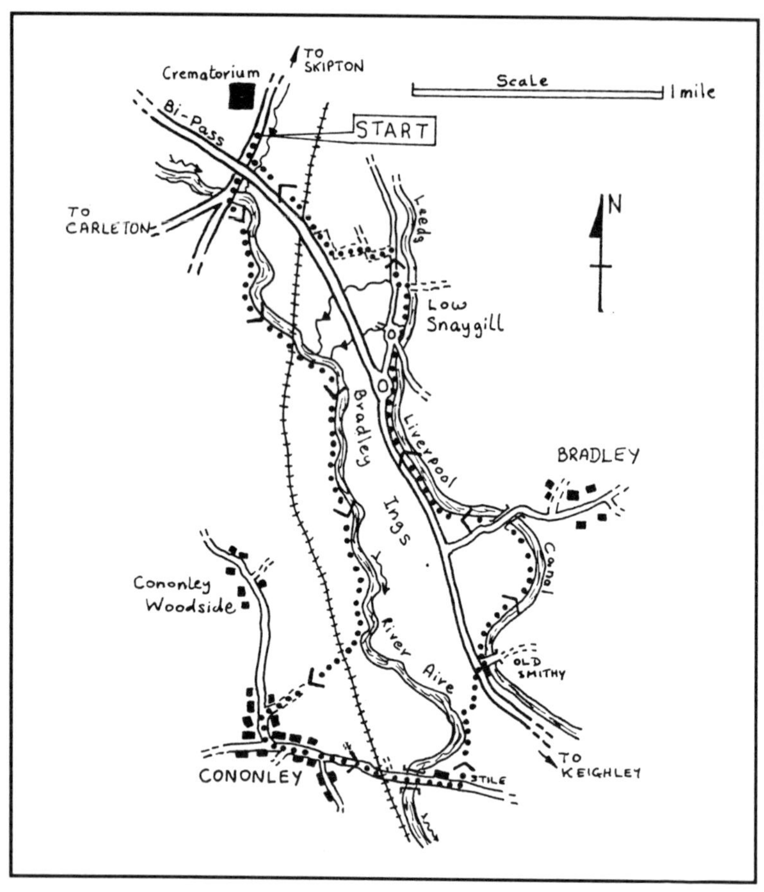

the Domesday Survey as Cutnelai, an Anglo-Saxon settlement where one Thorketell held two carucates of taxable land. The Canons of Bolton Priory later held one of their principal estates here too and this amounted to some 250 acres; however, it was probably the lead industry of the 19th century that made its mark on the village. For some time the lead mines gnawed into the sub-strata of Old Chy Gib, the rounded hill to the south of the village, and provided revenue for the owner, the Duke of Devonshire, and labour for the local population, though many mine workers were imported from the tin mines of Cornwall.

Cononley has a number of very interesting buildings, one of them being the Old Hall. This is situated close to the junction of Skipton Road with Main Street. The three-storey building has almost a chapel-like air about it and was long the residence of the Swire family. The oldest section of the building is the 17th century west side with its original mullion windows.

From the junction in the centre continue through Cononley, passing the village institute with its singular clock tower and the New Inn, and 50 yards afterwards alighting upon Milton House. This obviously old dwelling dates from the early 17th century and is reputed to have been constructed by the same builder responsible for Kildwick Hall. Looking at the ornate finial on the front edge of the left-hand gable the initial SE can be seen. The next building of any note is Pear Tree cottage 50 yards further along the road, located immediately opposite a bridge over the beck. This old farmhouse still boasts pegged oak doors and ornately carved rounded lintels.

Continue down Main Street now, passing the Railway public house to reach the level crossing where the Aire Valley line is once more crossed. Proceed along the road for quarter of a mile, crossing the river, and just after the mill here pick up a stile on the left (signposted Bradley). Descend the steps and follow the field path back to the riverbank, tracing this now for less than quarter of a mile to reach a fence and a hedgerow. There is a small streamlet running parallel to the latter at the far side. Turn right up the fence side to locate a stile in the wall corner. Cross the next pasture diagonally to a gap stile and the following field to yet another gap stile (gated) where the A629 is then joined.

The main road is crossed to walk up a track on the left side of an old delapidated house (formerly Craven Forge) to reach a bridge over the canal. Do not cross this, but instead turn left along the towpath, following the canal along its meandering course slightly west of Bradley village. Perhaps one-mile after the village the boat marina is reached at Low Snaygill. Walk beneath the bridge and continue for a further quarter of a mile to reach a swing bridge just after the Bay Horse Inn (refreshments). Leave the canal now, turning left from the bridge to reach the main road at the bottom.

Turn right along the A629 walking towards Skipton and crossing to the far side of the road. Take the first left turn that leads down into the Snaygill Industrial Estate and at the bottom turn right then left almost immediately, following a track running alongside the warehouse of Custom Built. This track is now traced towards Skipton by-pass seen ahead, and then followed around to the right. At the next bend just where the track ducks beneath the flyover look for and follow a path on the right beyond a stile.

The path now has a wall to the left and chain link fencing on the right until the railway banking is reached 50 yards ahead, where the path is then traced as it angles up to the right. Cross the line with care and descend again to a ladder stile. Now on field paths once more the right-of-way keeps to the left side of the following pastures until the footbridge over Eller Beck. Turn right now along Carleton Road to return to the starting point to complete the circuit.

WALK 8

SHARP HAW SUMMIT

Distance 7 miles. Expected duration three-and-a-half hours.

A moderate walk following field paths, exposed fells enjoying open views and forestry tracks.

The starting point is the top of Raikes Road close to the junction with Raikeswood Drive (three-quarters of a mile from town centre). Take a West Yorkshire bus (service Nos. 71, 72 or 809) to this point.

Landranger Map No. 103) is required for this walk.

FROM the road junction walk along the lane (signposted Stirton) with the shapely cone of Sharp Haw visible in the distance. After crossing the by-pass take the path down the banking on the right (waymarked with yellow arrows) and, after crossing a stile at the bottom, turn left to trace the fence alongside the road to another stile 100 yards later. After this is crossed a field path leads to another stile almost immediately, then with a line of trees to the left walk uphill to a wall corner at the top.

Ahead can be seen two thorn trees. Make for the right-hand of the two by a fence corner and from this point walk downhill heading for the far bottom corner adjacent to a caravan park. Pick up a stile here leading in rapid succession to another, after which a path is traced alongside the caravan park to the access avenue leading to Tarn House Hotel. Turn to the right and look for a yellow arrow fixed to a tree after 100 yards. This indicates the way left through an iron gate into the adjoining pasture. From here a diagonal uphill course passes between two mature trees to reach a ladder stile at the far side.

Turn right and walk up the lane for half-a-mile reaching a gate marked private at the fourth acute bend of the road. A fingerpost here indicates the bridleway to Flasby, an obvious track which is followed to a second fingerpost within half-a-mile. At this point take off half right along a less obvious line across open ground. As this heads across Skyrakes and Sharp Haw nears, the pathway becomes clear and over in the west Elslack Moor can be seen and beyond this the huge whaleback of Pendle Hill deep in the heart of Lancashire witch country.

Within striking distance of the summit, the bridleway takes off to the right and our route now follows an increasing gradient to a wall just below the top. A ladder stile is crossed here and the O.S. trig. point soon attained. Despite its modest elevation (1,160 ft) the hill represents one of the finest viewing points in the area. The 360 degree panorama stretches from the Upper Wharfedale fells of Buckden Pike and Great Whernside round over Malham Moor to Bowland and the hills previously mentioned. In the western foreground the canal can be seen winding its serpentine route through the village of Gargrave, whilst away in the south we see Skipton Moor with receding Airedale backed by the wind-swept moorlands of Brontë Country.

From the trig. point the well defined path continues downhill, but close to the foot of the slope trace a path away to the left passing a plantation on the right. The heathery way soon leads down to a gate in a wall corner. Pass through this and, now descending steeply, pass through a pine forest and thickets of rhododendrons to reach a fingerpost after quarter of a mile. Turn to the left here (signposted Bog Lane) along a forest trail which can be soft underfoot following rain. Soon a forestry road is met at a sweeping bend.

Turn left here (uphill) and follow the road through Crag Wood for one-and-a-half miles, the only views being afforded by the occasional firebreaks. The road levels out momentarily before descending past a junction to climb once more for a further quarter of a mile. Where the road bends around to the left look for and follow an obscure paths which leads off right down a banking to reach a gap stile in a dry-stone wall.

From this stile strike across the field due east to make for

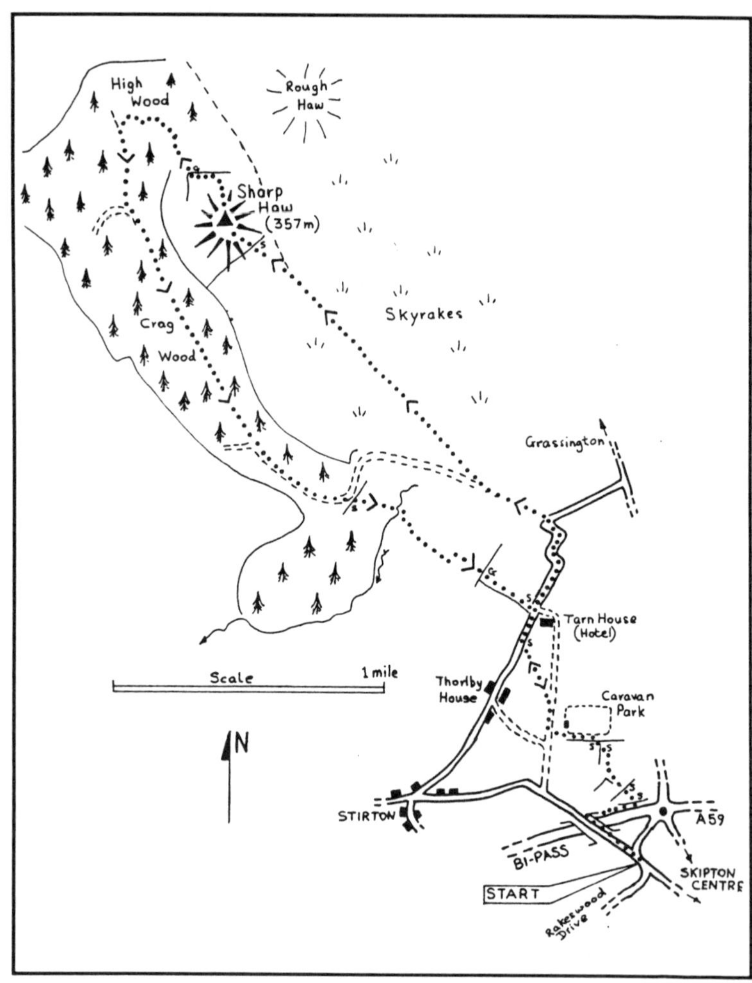

a gate hole and cross a small stream gulley on route. Pass through the gate and turn immediately right to follow the wall to another gate. Go through this and by keeping to the left-hand side of the pasture pass another stile at a wall corner. With a fence now on the left, walk along this until it can be negotiated by a stile, then by turning right and keeping to the right-hand edge of the next two fields once again enter the lane out of Stirton. A right turn here and the starting point can be reached by retracing our outward-bound route.

WALK 9

EASTBY AND BARDEN MOOR

Distance 8.25 miles. This route crosses the most exposed moorland described in this guide, the highest point reached being just below 1,400 ft. There are no particular difficulties with this walk so long as fine weather prevails; however, the walker must prepare himself for all eventualities. Apart from the track over Deer Gallows Plain and that leading from Eastby up to Hutchen Gill Head, all pathways are well defined and route finding should present no problems, provided the walker has map and compass and the ability to use them.

The route across these moors is subject to a statutory access agreement which provides for walkers to roam without hindrance subject to certain byelaws. Definitive paths excepted, there may be restrictions imposed for grouse shooting at certain times of the year. (Details may be obtained from National Park Centres or from the Estate Office, Bolton Abbey, tel. 227.) Allow 3-4 hours.

The most useful maps covering this walk are sheets SD 85/95 and SE 05/15 in the O.S. Pathfinder Series.

THE walk commences from Elm Tree Square in Embsay, easily reached by bus from Skipton (Pennine Bus Service No. 214 and West Yorkshire No. 276). The village is only ten minutes drive out of Skipton, car parking being available 80 yards east of the Elm Tree pub.

Leading directly from the car park, a ladder stile gives access to a field path running along a wall by a barn to reach a gap stile over to the right. From here the path runs for 60 yards between a wall and a wire fence to a further gap stile. At this point Embsay church can be seen in the trees over to the left. Follow the field path over to the far left corner and via a stile enter and turn left along the lane. Just past the church pick up a gap stile (gated) on the right and trace a tarmac path across the field to rejoin the lane further on.

Turn right here and walk into Eastby village, after quarter of a mile looking for a left turn into Hunters Croft (signposted Eastby Moor). Follow this right-of-way through the houses to find a stile at a fence, and from here trace a sunken pathway

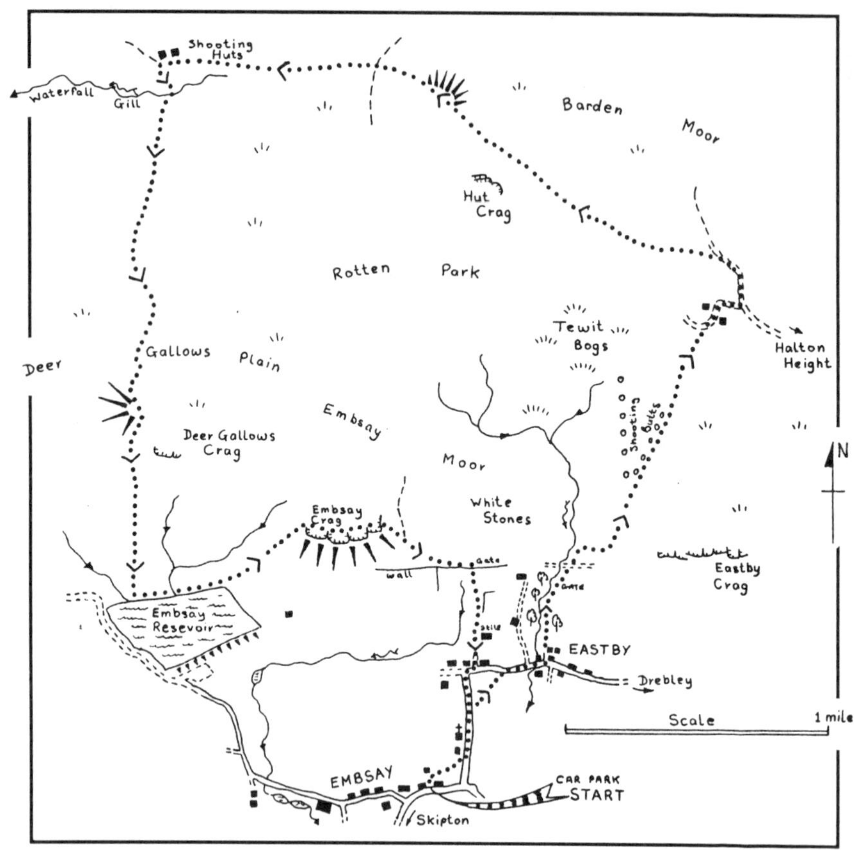

ascending through trees. Because of the tree cover this part of the route never dries out and in summer usually remains boggy underfoot. Up until the closing years of the 19th century, stone and a poor grade coal was delved for on the moor and sledged down the hillsides. This mode of transport accounts for the sunken appearance of this and some other tracks in the vicinity.

The leafy tunnel eventually leads the walker to another stile where the path then breaks out into the open with views of Eastby Crag to the east. Still climbing the path keeps to the left-hand wall reaching a stile after 120 yards. Here a farm track cuts across at right angles, but by negotiating another stile ahead the open moor beckons. The waters of Heugh Gill can at this point be heard but not seen as it runs through a wooded cleft down to the left. Very soon however the wall on the left makes an acute turn and the ravine can then be seen.

The path now clings to the eastern edge of the stream valley as it wends its way on an ever steepening course. After 200 yards an old boundary stone is reached near a clump of rushes, but just before this is a gate with a ladder stile is reached. With Heugh Gill left to carve out its course from Tewitt Bogs, turn right over this stile and walk up the left side of the next pasture, passing through the following gate and then heading for the top left corner and a ladder stile. The open moor is now in front and a very indistinct route leads off towards Hutchen Gill Head.

The best way forward is to strike a course slightly east of north, over the rise to where two lines of shooting butts may be seen crossing the moors. At the first butt ignore the ones going straight forward, but head off along those angling away at a tangent. The path quickly becomes more obvious until, when the last butt is reached and Lower Barden Reservoir comes into view, the route is easily followed downhill towards two shelters 80 yards in front.

From these huts a track winds down to meet the bridleway linking Halton Height with Rylstone. This is the definitive route across Barden Moor, and one which tradition says the fabled white doe made its weekly visit from Rylstone to Bolton Priory.

Turn left now following the bridleway in a north-westerly direction heading for Brown Bank Brow, slowly ascending along a good track. Over to the right at a distance of five miles can be seen the twin tops of Simon's Seat and Earl Seat. About 150 yards after first meeting the bridleway a track cut across at right angles and a marker post stands at the junction. This route contours along the fell towards Upper Barden Reservoir and our way is by keeping to the main track, soon levelling out at Brown Bank one mile ahead.

Soon the notched skyline of Rylstone Fell and Cracoe Fell can be seen in front with the obelisk at Watt Crag plainly seen. A fingerpost is reached (signposted Eastby) pointing out a route which descends via Rotten Park to Embsay and Eastby villages. Continuing forward the track cuts a swathe through heather moors which are best seen in mid-August to early September when the flowers are in bloom. After three-quarters of a mile two turf-roofed shooting huts stand close to a junction of routes. Ahead the bridleway continues its descent to join the old coach road into Rylstone, whilst our route leads off to the left, crossing the infant Waterfall Gill before climbing over East Harts Hill and Embsay Moor.

Following a climb of almost a mile the pathway levels out then begins a winding descent over Deer Gallow Plain. The view from this point is fine indeed with Embsay and Skipton occupying the foreground and the Aire Valley stretching away past Rivock Edge. As altitude is lost Embsay Reservoir comes into view and over to the right the point where Crookrise Top drops into Nettlehole Wood is marked by a few stunted trees on the fell edge.

As the way down steepens, a rock outcrop can be seen over to the left known as Deer Gallows and beyond is the rising wedge of Embsay Crag. At the foot of the hill a bridleway is met where it runs along the north side of the reservoir. Turning left along this, walk for 200 yards to where a footbridge spans a feeder stream, and then take the steep way that winds up through deep bracken to the summit of Embsay Crag. A continuation of the track is less steep as it drops down to and follows an enclosure wall.

After passing a sheepfold turn right through the second gate (look for the yellow paint spot) where the pathway down over Rotten Park joins from the left. Keeping to the right wall side, head for the bottom of the field where a green lane continues and a beck flows in a ravine down on the right. Soon a stile is met by a farm, after which the access track descends rapidly to meet the road between Embsay and Eastby at the acute corner. Turn to the right and an easy stroll of half-a-mile returns the walker to the starting point.

WALK 10

CANAL ROUTE TO GARGRAVE AND ROMAN VILLA

Distance 9 miles. Level going all the way for which 3-4 hours should be allowed. Pleasant walking along the Leeds to Liverpool Canal leads to the half-way halt at Gargrave, followed by a return along field paths taking in the site of a Roman antiquity.

The recommended map is Landranger Series sheet No. 103.

THIS walk can be started at either the railway station car park in Broughton Road or at Belmont Bridge in the town centre. In either instance the canal towpath is followed as far as Holme Bridge on the outskirts of Gargrave and some five-and-a-half miles from Skipton.

After passing beneath the bridge and climbing the steps on the left, continue along the towpath instead of crossing the locks by the footbridge. An especially picturesque section of canal follows as far as Ray Bridge quarter of a mile distant, with colour being provided by yellow flag lilies when in season (June). A further quarter of a mile brings the walker to the next bridge where the Eshton and Malham road crosses adjacent to a caravan park.

Walk up the incline on the left and cross Eshton Road, leaving the canalside pathway in favour of a footpath which skirts a residential area. This path is reached by way of an iron gate to trace this right-of-way to where it intersects a quiet cul-de-sac and within 60 yards then meets North Street. Turn to the left here and 50 yards later bear right and walk along Main Street into the village centre. Cross the road towards the bridge over the river Aire which is located close to an ancient ford. With plenty of shops for refreshments the idyllic surroundings at this point make the centre of the village an ideal half-way halt.

From the river bridge stroll along Church Street (signposted railway station and Broughton) as far as the church which is dedicated to St. Andrew. Gargrave is without doubt a settlement of some antiquity since the Domesday entry for Geregraue shows that there was then a holding of three carucates of land taxable. Very little of earlier structures has survived, with the oldest part of the present church being the tower which is believed to date from about the early 16th century. The remainder of the building was rebuilt in 1852 during which a number of stones were unearthed apparently dating from Saxon times. The base of a Norman pillar was also found.

The old Gargrave Manor House would appear to have been sited on land known locally as Garris Close and stood a few yards on the west side of the road from the church past the railway station. Here we can still see evidence of a moat that one presumes surrounded the building. Other interesting buildings in the village are a cottage in South Street where local poet Robert Story once lived and the Old Hall where tradition has it Cromwell stayed during the siege of Skipton Castle.

After examining the church, turn down Church Lane (east) passing the site of Goffa Mill, now converted to residential purposes, and when the tarmac lane peters out continue along the track to where this divides close to the village common. Here a public footpath branches off on the right (signed). Follow this past farm buildings to the right and about quarter of a mile out of the village pick up a ladder stile on the right where the track makes a left turn.

Once over the stile turn left to pass through a gap in the wall ahead, and after this and walking more or less parallel with the railway located to the right, make for a gap in the fence at the far end of the pasture. Kirk Sink House is now located over to the left and probably stands close to the site of another of the seven chapels with which, according to tradition, the Parish of Gargrave was endowed prior to the ravages of the Scots during the 13th century. A few yards on the north-west side of Kirk Sink is the site of a Roman villa, though all that now remains are a few meaningless undulations.

Once through the gap in the fence make for the far right corner of the next field and here pick up a ladder stile. Cross this and walk through a gate on the right five yards beyond, to trace an overgrown pathway along the foot of the railway embankment to a gate after 150 feet. A farm track here swings under the railway; however, the route is straight forward, initially along the line of some trees. A field barn can be seen ahead, to the right of which is a gate hole through which the route passes. From here strike across the next pasture towards a gate in the far right-hand wall corner and, with the wall on the right, proceed now until after half-a-mile from leaving the barn the way forward turns right beneath the railway to a gate.

Climbing slightly from this point with a wall now to the left, pick up a stile in the top left corner, cross the wall and for the following three-quarters of a mile keep to the right-hand wall at the top of the next two pastures. The wall eventually swings around to meet two gates on the right with a farm visible not too far beyond. Ignore these gates, however, to continue straight forward, this time along a fence. From here the busy A59 can be seen about three-quarters of a mile ahead. Some quarter of a mile after the bend by the twin gates the rail bridge spanning the river Aire is then almost immediately to the left. Here the fence one has been tracing gives way to an isolated section of dry-stone walling with a stile.

Although an obvious pathway continues, cross at the stile

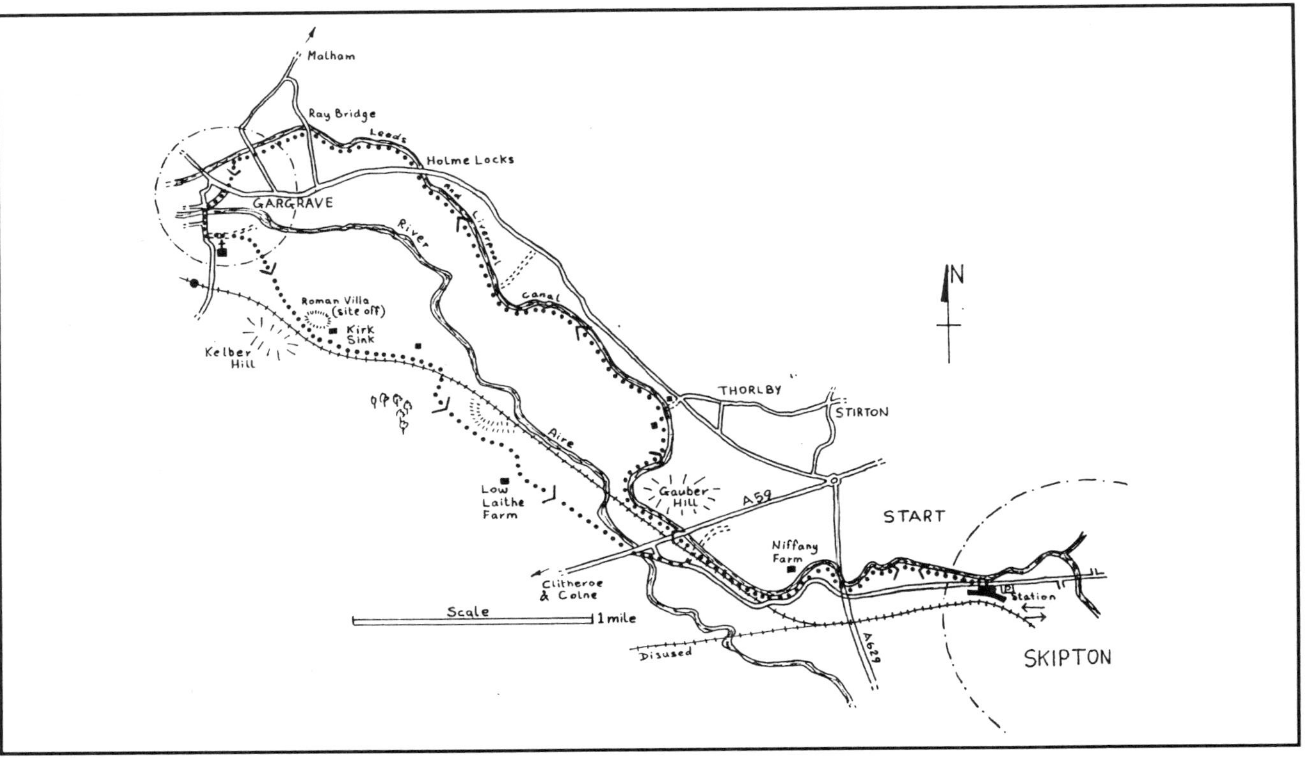
Malham
Ray Bridge
Leeds
Holme Locks
And
Liverpool
Canal
GARGRAVE
River
Aire
Roman Villa (site off)
Kirk Sink
Kelber Hill
N
THORLBY
STIRTON
Gauber Hill
A59
Low Laithe Farm
START
Niffany Farm
Clitheroe & Colne
Station
Scale
1 mile
Disused
A629
SKIPTON

and then turn left to follow a course that cuts across the left-hand angle of the field to reach a stile at a fence running parallel to the main road. After ascending the embankment cross the road with care, and at the opposite side pick and follow the overgrown course of the former road alignment as this spans the river at the old bridge. When the used section of the road is again met, bear right and after 180 yards take the first left down to a gate. The railway level crossing is soon reached, beyond which a gated stile half right from the track leads to an ascending footpath quickly joining the towpath along the canal. The starting point is now easily reached by retracing our outward-bound route back to Skipton.

WALK 11

LOTHERSDALE

Distance 9 miles.

This route involves a few steep gradients and sections that are muddy following heavy rain. Average parties should allow about five-and-a-half hours for the walk through this interesting valley. The starting point is the car park and popular viewpoint on Elslack Moor (SD 939473) beside the moor road from Colne to Skipton, some five miles west of the latter.

Recommended maps are the Landranger Series sheet No. 103 and Pathfinder Map SD 84/94.

LOTHERSDALE follows a brief course of some five miles before opening into the Aire Valley close to Kildwick, and due to its former isolation was fortunate to escape the attention of the 14th century Scottish raids and the Luddites of the early 19th century. The earliest reference to the dale is found in the Domesday Survey of 1086 when it was then called Lodresdene meaning valley of beggars. The etymology of this name is derived from the Old English lodder meaning beggar and the Anglicised form of the Norse component "-dal" for valley. The first true settlers were undoubtedly Anglo-Saxon in origin, although the Nordic influence is self-evident in many place-names. At the time of the Norman Conquest the Saxon thane Gamall is on record as having ten carucates of taxable land in Lodresdene.

Embarking upon this route which practically covers the entire length of Lothersdale, turn west along the road from the car parking area, to a junction after 150 yards. Here the Pennine Way cuts across the road. Turn to the left up the stony track, following this eventually around a left-hand bend and gradually ascending to the O.S. trig. point on Pinhaw Beacon, the highest point along the walk at 1,261 ft. From here a magnificent view unfolds northwards across the Aire Gap to the soft lines of the Yorkshire Dales and, when the air is clear, to the rugged peaks of the Lake District over 30 miles distant.

Leaving Pinhaw, follow the Pennine Way along a well-beaten path, tracing this downhill to a wall where by bearing to the left along this and around a corner to the right a step stile is met. A field path follows for 70 yards to enter a lane leading to Hewitt's Farm. Walk downhill to the tarmac road, cross the stile immediately in front and, with a wall on the left, quickly reach another stile. At this point the Pennine Way strikes off to the right; however, by continuing straight forward towards a line of power cables a descent is affected into a stream gulley. Cross this and follow the overgrown and often boggy track uphill to where it joins into a farm track.

Still ascending, walk up the track to the sharp left-hand bend to find a stile on the right a few yards before. With the wall on your left trace the vague field path to a wall corner, proceed around this and aim for the gate at the far end. Note that the right-hand gate post is in fact an old milestone reading Settle 11 miles and Keighley 5 miles. Turn right here and stroll along the road for half-a-mile, turning right at the first cross-roads and not far ahead pick up a stile on the left opposite the first farm house. Follow the field path heading for the bottom left extremity of the wood to pick up a gap stile followed immediately by a rickety ladder stile.

After cautiously negotiating this suspect stile the route ahead follows first a wall, then a line of hawthorn trees indicates the way forward to an iron gate and from there passing between Leys House. Walk through the yard and once again pick up the continuing field path beyond a further stile and then follow this now for about half-a-mile to Cook House. Ahead may be seen the sweep of Sutton Moor and the gritstone edge of Earl Crag. As Cook House nears, aim for a gate to the left of the buildings to discover a double stile leading the walker around the rear of a chicken shed and out into a lane. Turn right along this to a stile on the left after 40 yards, and follow the path

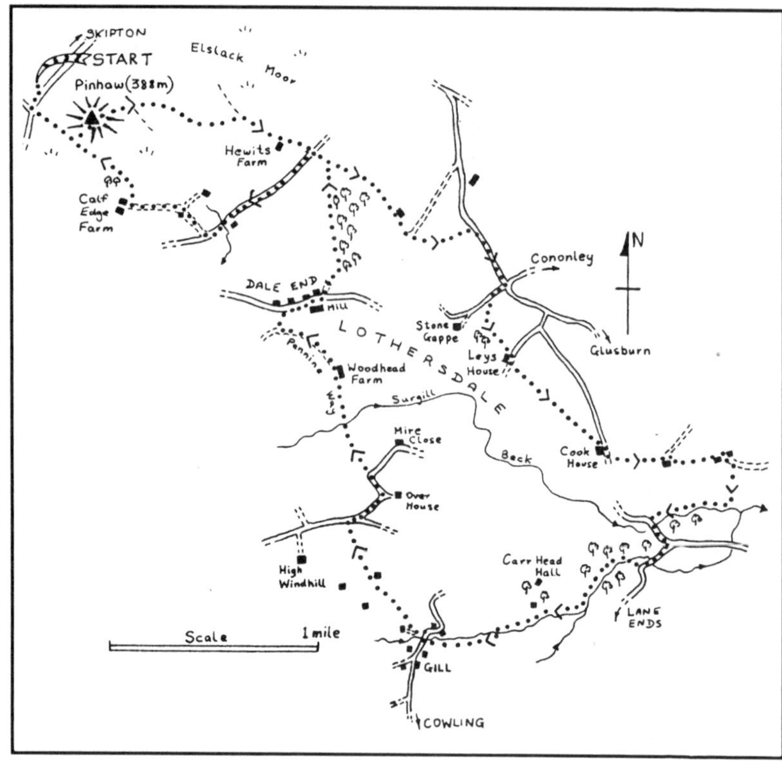

for quarter of a mile through pastures to another farmstead. this is passed on its left side to another stile and a gate quickly followed by yet another stile over to the left. From here keep to the top edge of the following field until the next wall is met then make for a gate adjacent to the next farm.

When the farm is reached walk between the buildings into the yards, and turn to the left out through a gate to bear sharp right. In the bottom corner of the field are two gates. Ignoring the one to the right, carry on forward down an overgrown track soon bearing right along Surgill Beck. At this point route finding is less clear, but by tracing the beck upstream as far as a vegetated gully, turn right up this to find a partially concealed footbridge. Beyond this a well-defined field path can be followed to the next stile by a gate. Enter the lane here turning left over the bridge and around a left-hand bend. A stile to the right leads to an extremely narrow gap stile reached via a short but steep path and a few nettle-infested stone steps. After negotiating these hazards turn left along the lane to reach a junction within a matter of yards.

Turn right here and walk downhill to where a bridge and bend follow in rapid succession and a footbridge is reached on the right. Cross Lumb Mill Beck to follow the bank of the stream along a path soon developing into a pleasant woodland walk. About half-a-mile afterwards a gate is reached; however, nearby just before this can be seen a lime kiln of unusual design, one of numerous relics of an industrial past no longer with us. At various times during the history of the valley, lead, barytes and coal have all been mined here while lime burning took place and stone was quarried for local building work.

Passing through the gate and keeping to the right bank of the beck, the latter meanders through ash dominated broad-leafed woodlands to another gate and a footbridge. Do not cross here but carry on forward until the next bridge is met, crossing at this point to trace field paths uphill for a little less than a mile. The tiny hamlet of Gill is now entered and the Pennine Way rejoined. Turn to the right in Gill and, when the lane divides, bear right down to a bridge taking the first left once over the beck. At the end of the track just before the house, a gate on the right gives way to a field path climbing steeply by way of Stubbing. After three-quarters mile of this the moor lane from high Windhill to Cowling Hill is entered. This road follows the course of the old Colne to Addingham turnpike which was the main link between these two towns until 1809.

As if travelling to Cowling Hill, turn right along the lane, still on the Pennine Way, and at the very first junction turn left. From here the road zig-zags down towards Mire Close, but it is left for a field path at the second bend where a fingerpost indicates the way northwards. Away across the dale to the north-east can be seen the imposing country mansion of Stone Gappe, where in 1839 Charlotte Brontë was employed as governess.

After leaving the lane behind, a path wends its way down the hill through two gates to cross Surgill Beck at a ford, then a short but stiff climb takes the walker to Woodhead Farm. Note the sundial and engraved tablet set into the southern gable. Walk along the farm track to where at a left bend Dale End comes into view. A fingerpost here directs Pennine travellers forward down the hill, to enter the hamlet a few yards west of the Hare and Hounds pub, a welcome refreshment halt if the weather is hot.

Opposite the public house is a car park built in 1964 on the site of the pinfold, a fact now marked by a plaque. To the left of the car park down between terraced cottages can be found the mill, now the base of a local pine furniture business. It appears that a mill of one sort or another has existed here since at least Norman times, and in the rent rolls belonging to the Cliffords of Skipton, an entry for the year 1603 refers to a George Tillotson who paid 31 shillings for a tenement in Lothersdale and 6s 8d for a water corn mill. In later years a successful cotton spinning operation was also established and the present mill building still houses one of the country's largest indoor water wheels.

To continue northwards now, turn left up the lane to the east of the Hare and Hounds just beyond the barn, and after walking up this a few yards turn the bend to reach a gate. Turn left here and walk up the fence side initially then along a wall that draws the walker into a corner where a stile is located and the outward bound route is once again joined. Turning to the left here the lane is quickly reached, but instead of heading straight forward up the lane leading to Hewitt's Farm, turn left and follow the road for half-a-mile.

Where a lane leads off at a tangent on the right shortly beyond a dip in the road, leave the latter and head for Calf Edge Farm. When the track divides by a ruined barn bear left and look for a gap stile on the right just before the farm buildings. Take the field path, heading for a gate and stile in the top wall, and still climbing strike out for the top edge of a group of trees seen over to the left where another stile is crossed. The heather moors are with us once again from this point and the summit of Pinhaw is now to be seen ahead. From the stile the moorland path is now traced back to the Pennine Way at a wall corner from where five minutes strolling returns to the starting point.

USEFUL ADDRESSES AND TELEPHONE NUMBERS

The Yorkshire Dales National Park, Colvend, Hebden Road, Grassington. Tel: 0756-752748.

The Countryside Commission, John Dower House, Crescent Place, Cheltenham, Glos., GL50 3RA. Tel: 0242-521381.

Yorkshire and Humberside Tourist Board, 312 Tadcaster Road, York, YO2 2HF. Tel: 0904-707961.

Upper Wharfedale Museum Society, 6 The Square, Grassington. Tel: 0756-752800.

The Ramblers' Association, 1-5 Wandsworth Road, London, SW8 2XX. Tel: 01-582 6878.

Pennine Motor Services (buses), Grouse Garage, Gargrave. Tel: 075 678-215.

Skipton Town Council, Town Hall, High Street, Skipton. Tel: 0756-4357.

Snaygill Boats, The Moorings, Skipton Road, Snaygill. Tel: 0756-795150.

Craven Herald and Pioneer, 36 High Street, Skipton. Tel: 0756-794117.

Pennine Boat Trips, The Wharfe, Waterside Court, Skipton. Tel: 0756-790829.

Council for National Parks, 45 Shelton Street, London, WC2H 9HJ. Tel: 01-240 3603.

Yorkshire Dales Railway (steamers), Embsay Station, Skipton. Tel: 0756-794727.

Craven Museum, Town Hall, Skipton. Tel: 0756-794079.

British Tourist Authority/English Tourist Board, Thames Tower, Black's Road, London, W6 9EL. Tel: 01-846 9000.

Ancient Monuments Commission, (Dept. of the Environment), 25 Saville Row, London, W1X 2BT.

Forestry Commission (North Yorks.), 1a Grosvenor Terrace, York, YO3 7BD.

North Yorkshire County Council, County Hall, Northallerton. Tel: 0609-780780.

Nature Conservancy Council, Archbold House, Archbold Terrace, Newcastle-upon-Tyne, NE2 1EG. Tel: 091-2816316.

Yorkshire Wildlife Trust, 10 Toft Green, York, YO1 1JT. Tel: 0904-59570.

Yorkshire Water Authority, West Riding House, 67 Albion Street, Leeds, LS1 5AA. Tel: 0532-448201.

Woodland Trust, Westgate, Grantham, Lincolnshire, NG31 6LL.

The Ordnance Survey, Romsey Road, Maybush, Southampton, SO9 4DH.

Balloon Flights. Tel: 0756-752937.

Steam Train Information. Tel: 0756-795189.

Footpath Difficulties. Tel: 0756-793344.

Tourist Information Centres:
Grassington, Pletts Barn. Tel: 0756-753083.
Skipton, Victoria Square. Tel: 0756-792809.

Skipton Castle. Tel: 0756-792442.

Youth Hostel Association. Tel: 0756 752400.

Taxis:
Marina Taxis. Tel: 0756-794757.
Moorview Taxis. Tel: 0756-793105.
Skipton Private Hire. Tel: 0756-794994.